SMALL BUSINESS TAXES

The Complete Guide for Businesses and Self-Employed to Save Money, Avoid IRS Penalties, and Increase Your Net Profit

THOMAS WATSON

Table of Contents

Introduction

As an entrepreneur you are aware of the tasks required to run a small company. Marketing, operations, customer service and strategic planning all pose challenges. Among these responsibilities taxes have the potential to make or break your business.

The success of your company hinges on your ability to navigate the complexities of taxation which is an aspect of any organization. However, as a business owner wearing hats can make it challenging to become an expert, in the intricate world of taxes. The content provided in "The Small Business Guide to Taxes" aims to empower you with confidence in making tax decisions and equip you with an edge for success.

This comprehensive guide aims to demystify the tax code by explaining concepts in simple language. It offers information and advice that will allow you to optimize your tax planning efforts, reduce obligations and ensure compliance with all legal requirements—whether you operate as a sole proprietorship, partnership, LLC, or corporation.

Drawing upon the expertise of accountants and consultants specialized in assisting businesses with their tax matters, this inclusive handbook serves as a resource for navigating tax related challenges.

We will not rest until we have done everything to simplify the tax system from understanding corporate taxation to grasping the tax implications of different company structures.

The book covers tax deductions and credits for businesses well as emphasizes the importance of maintaining detailed records and submitting forms on time. It also gives advice on how to minimize your tax bill within legal limits via careful tax planning.

Furthermore, the book acknowledges that tax laws are subject to changes. It explains how new tax legislation will impact businesses emphasizing the significance of staying up to date with the developments in tax law and adapting your approach accordingly. The objective is to provide you with the tools you need to make educated choices about the financial future of your business.

Remember that taxes are both a burden and an opportunity for savings. By conducting some research and careful planning you can take advantage of tax benefits designed specifically for businesses. You will be able to use those resources to grow your business and go after your dreams.

So, turn the page reader if you are ready to delve into the intricacies of tax management, to safeguard the financial future of your small business.

Utilize "The Small Business Guide, to Taxes," as a resource that can steer you towards a law-abiding business venture.

Chapter 1
A Primer on Taxes for Local Enterprise

Business taxation encompasses the taxes that businesses are obligated to pay as a part of their operations. Regardless of whether you are a proprietor, a partner, part of a liability company or even a corporation it is vital for your business to comply with tax regulations. Diverse types of businesses entail tax implications. It is crucial to consider both the tax related aspects and non-tax considerations of your business to determine the entity that will facilitate its growth and succession planning for future generations.

1.1 The Basics of Taxation for Businesses

Businesses must pay attention to five different tax categories:

- tax for Excise
- tax for corporate franchise
- tax Gross-receipts
- tax Employment withholding
- VAT (Value-added tax)

Taxes on earnings, assets, and transactions all fall within this category. The mining and insurance sectors, among others, are subject to taxes, though. Although these taxes may not be categorized as "business taxes " they still have an impact on individuals as they affect people personally.

Tax Liability

As a business owner you have the responsibility of managing expenses, including taxes, for your business. The government enforces taxation on aspects of your company. The amount you owe federal, state, and local governments is known as your tax obligation. The government uses this funding to help finance events and services.

It is important to note that tax liability is a binding debt that must be paid within a year; failure to do so may result in penalties imposed by the government. In your accounting workbook or balance sheet short term liabilities, like tax liability can be recorded together.

Any transaction that carries a tax consequence is known as an " event." The government holds the authority to determine which events fall under this category. Whenever such an event occurs within your business it becomes necessary to pay the associated tax authority. Taxable events include income, payroll processing and sales activities. Each taxable event attracts varying amounts of tax liability calculated as a percentage of the event.

When you sell a product, it becomes an event for which the government may require you to collect sales tax.

If using your money to pay for sales tax, you have the option to incorporate the tax amount into the total price you change your customers. Once you have collected the sales tax it is important to report it and submit it to the government agencies. You can choose to pay sales tax monthly. It is worth noting that earning income is also subject to taxation. Your federal and state income tax obligations are calculated based on a percentage of your earned income.

Calculating Business Taxes

Understanding the ins and outs of tax processes is crucial, whether it is, for business transactions. As a business owner and taxpayer, it is important to know the time and method to perform these transactions to minimize your tax obligations legally. Remember, while it is wise to minimize taxes, evading them through hiding or deception is illegal.

Any costs related to the operation of a "trade or business" may be deducted from your taxable income. This refers to doing things with the goal of gaining financial gain. According to IRS guidelines, a trade or company must include action and the expectation of financial gain.

Your income year should coincide with the fiscal year in which you file your taxes. Every penny. All income. Accrued within a year must be reported in that year's tax return alongside any relevant expenses paid or accrued. It is important to apply any tax saving strategies before the end of the tax year.

Additionally, you will need to disclose your chosen accounting method to the IRS. The two primary methods commonly used by business owners are "cash" and "accrual." In situations there may be opportunities for utilizing an approach that combines elements from both methods.

Furthermore, specific types of businesses might have the opportunity to utilize accounting techniques.

1.2 Benefits of Tax Knowledge for Decisions

Some organizations thoroughly analyze business cases to assist with investment decisions. They often only consider tax figures in their calculations. On the hand some organizations understand the complete cost involved in acquiring new fixed assets, but they may lack clarity regarding the amount and timing of potential tax rebates related to such purchases. Furthermore, transnational companies sometimes make choices based on division performance without considering the effect of cross-border transactions and taxes.

Traditionally tax considerations have been seen as an afterthought once a business decision has been made. This approach is due to knowledge about tax calculations. Often overlooks the possibility of significant negative cash impacts resulting from increased taxes that could undermine the anticipated savings or benefits of the business decision.

However, incorporating tax planning into business decisions helps ensure an understanding of cash benefits and prevents costly issues from arising. It also facilitates implementation of processes for managing intercompany transactions supporting the business decision while ensuring that necessary data is gathered effectively to meet tax requirements.

Transfer pricing and other specific tax considerations

Let us look at three specific types of taxes—research and development tax credits, capital allowances, and transfer pricing—that might impact business decisions. Businesses can claim R&D tax rebates and capital allowances for expenses as a way for HMRC to encourage investments.

Depending on the type of investment a company makes, making an R&D or capital allowance claim could mean recovering, then 100% of the investment cost within one year of incurring the expenditure. This has an impact when considering cost-benefit analysis.

Transfer pricing ensures that each country receives the amount of tax when organizations engage in border transactions between their own entities. This is achieved by aligning profits with the value generating activities performed by entities ensuring that intercompany prices are comparable to those negotiated between parties.

The OECD's Inclusive Framework on Base Erosion & Profit Shifting (BEPS) has fostered a growing agreement on transfer pricing laws. This framework builds upon commonly adopted or referenced guidelines provided by the OECD regarding transfer pricing rules. Has been signed by 135 countries at present.

This agreement is valuable when attempting to strategize intercompany transactions as it provides some assurance on how to establish and uphold transfer pricing policies. However, it also implies that inadequate planning is more likely to result in tax audits and potential cash tax expenses which can harm the business situation.

Business decision-making through Transfer pricing & tax

Tax considerations are becoming increasingly integral to business decision-making. When businesses adopt models, such as work for executives, there can be additional compliance costs, changes in tax rates applied to profits and expenses incurred in documenting the adjustments made to the business model.

Regional centralization of warehousing

Let us take an example of a group planning to shift their operations to a warehousing model in Poland. This move aims to cater to customers in mainland Europe from divisions located in Poland, Germany, France, and the UK. This change was made to take advantage of economies of scale and cut down on expenses. These factors have been considered while evaluating the feasibility of the move; however, these evaluations are based on tax, profit, and loss forecasts.

It is important to carefully analyze the plan's tax consequences before committing to it. Initially it would be prudent to explore what types of capital allowances are available or foregone due to the change in warehouse location. As these directly impact the viability of this project. Additionally practical decisions regarding transfer pricing will need consideration.

One such weighty decision is determining who will legally own the inventory stored at the warehouse.

There might be some establishing concerns if the existing owners (Poland, France, Germany, and the United Kingdom) opt to maintain ownership. As a result, the UK company would be judged to be operating in Poland and would be liable for taxes there. Additionally, there could be complications regarding VAT registration. To sell its wares in Poland, the UK company would have to register for and pay value-added tax there.

On the hand if the stock is transferred to the entity it would result in tax charges like VAT and customs duties.

Assuming stock transfer is decided upon, a full transfer price study would be required. This analysis will determine the functions, assets and risks associated with centralizing warehousing activities. Consequently, it will establish a price for transactions between the entity and entities in the UK/France/Germany. These determinations will have an impact on tax calculations made by tax authorities in each jurisdiction.

It is important to consider that engaging in these tax-related tasks may offset some of the benefits gained from centralizing warehouse operations.

Investment in an innovative production facility

When companies consider expanding, they often need to invest in production lines. The cost benefit analysis of these lines focuses on projected revenue and the ability to manufacture products efficiently aiming for pretax profits.

However, it is important to note that these business cases sometimes overlook the option of capital allowances and R&D tax credits, which can make the case more compelling. Capital allowances allow companies to receive tax relief on their investment by deducting it from their income. This reduces the amount of cash they must pay as taxes, improving cash flow predictions and positively impacting the tax profit and loss statement.

Likewise, if the new production line involves research and development activities there may be opportunities for R&D tax credits. These credits help mitigate a company's tax liability and in situations may even result in payable tax credits being awarded to the business. Again, this boosts cash flow forecasts. Has the potential to enhance both pre- and post-tax profit and loss positions.

An additional process burdens.

One factor that is often overlooked is the level of complexity involved in implementing process changes to address tax compliance issues stemming from a business decision. While most businesses typically consider the impact on their accounting systems and processes, they tend to overlook the implications for tax compliance in relation to transfer pricing. This omission may add complexity to systems and expenses to ensure tax compliance.

In a warehousing scenario it is likely that management will need to evaluate the warehouse's performance and keep track of details for tax authorities. If costs and revenues are monitored without incorporating transfer pricing rules there is a risk of tracking two sets of numbers: one for management reporting and another for reporting. This does not prove costly and time-consuming but also introduces complexities when reconciling.

The recommended approach is to adopt an allocation method while considering its impact on management performance metrics and evaluating changes required.

While taxes should never be the driving factor, behind business decisions it is crucial to consider them. It is highly advisable to incorporate the tax impact into cost analysis, benefit assessment and cash flow forecasts.

Tax pros in demand

CPAs might expect strong job prospects. Find most of their work in companies and accountancy firms. At accounting firms tax professionals often collaborate with clients throughout the day. Unlike auditors, who follow a career path in accounting, tax accountants can take a stance for their clients.

According to Edwards, "As their advocate, you're essentially saying, 'We will choose the option for you within the boundaries of tax laws and provide support and defense for it.'"

On the side tax professionals focus on a business entity and become experts in addressing the specific tax challenges faced by that company and its industry. The extent of their responsibilities often varies based on the size of the company's tax department.

In companies individual tax accountants may specialize in areas like state and local sales taxes while working as part of a larger tax team. In companies a small group of individuals or one person may manage all state and federal taxes.

Tax accountants have career opportunities due to their understanding of taxes, which play a significant role in every business decision made by a company. This positions them well to advance to roles within an organization such as CFO or leading mergers and acquisitions efforts.

"According to Edwards it's important to have an understanding and appreciation for taxes no matter what your goals are. It can greatly benefit you in many ways."

Tax Traits

Determining if tax is the right for you involves conducting research, comprehending applications, and analyzing financial implications. Tax experts must familiarize themselves with their clients' businesses and industries to understand how tax regulations are relevant in those contexts.

According to an expert completing a tax return can be likened to solving a research question—a gratifying endeavor for individuals who enjoy unraveling puzzles. It is intellectually stimulating and presents challenges.

Finding solutions to tax related issues does not offer a sense of fulfillment. Also mirrors the satisfaction derived from solving intricate crossword puzzles or Sudoku boards. Tax professionals strive to leverage the rules within boundaries to benefit their clients.

Competence is essential, but so is the ability to express oneself clearly in writing and in person. As pointed out by the expert, tax professionals work alongside accountants as part of a team fostering collaboration while regularly interacting with individuals throughout the organization they are assisting.

Taking the next step

Being a tax expert calls for a wide range of knowledge and experience. The good news is that you can embark on a tax career in one year by pursuing a Master of Accounting degree (MAC). You have the option to earn UNCs MAC through either an, on campus program or an online program offering flexibility to learn at your pace. Many graduates of the MAC program continue collaborating with their employer but benefit from a faster career progression due to their enhanced understanding of finance, accounting, and taxation. Regardless of the program format you choose you will receive the regarded degree from UNC, gain access to a strong alumni network and receive support from career services, for resume polishing, interview preparation and connecting with potential employers.

1.3 Overview of Key Tax Types

Most individuals primarily focus on state income taxes. However, business owners must consider five tax categories that may be part of their responsibilities.

1. Income taxes; As per the IRS guidelines all businesses, except for partnerships, are required to file an income tax return. Partnerships need to file an information return. It is essential to note that individual income tax returns using IRS Form 1040 must also be filed every year.
2. Income tax on wages not subject to withholding & self-employment tax are two examples of taxes for which you will often need to make anticipated tax payments. You may have to pay a penalty if your projected tax payments do not cover your whole tax bill.
3. Self-employment taxes: This tax applies to proprietors,

general partners and typically members of liability companies (LLCs). It covers Social Security and Medicare taxes.

4. Employment taxes: If you have employees working for your business you must report and deposit income tax withholding well as Social Security and Medicare (FICA) taxes (where both the employee and employer contribute) along, with Federal Unemployment (FUTA) tax.

5. Sales taxes: Businesses might have an obligation to collect sales taxes on their transactions and remit them to their states or other states where they operate.

Dealing with business related taxation can become intricate. Small business owners often seek the expertise of tax professionals to assist them with tax strategies and filing requirements. It is essential to understand the tax system and business tax obligations so that you can effectively collaborate with your tax professional and make the most out of opportunities.

A Special Gift for Our Readers!

Dear Esteemed Reader,

Thank you for selecting this book. Your choice honors us, and we are excited to be part of your educational and professional journey.

We believe in providing value beyond the pages you hold in your hands. To enhance your learning experience, we have curated exclusive content tailored to complement and enrich the insights shared in this book.

Unlock a World of Exclusive Insights!

By scanning the QR code below, you will unveil a treasure trove of additional resources, tips, and expert insights, meticulously crafted to empower your learning journey.

Dive Deeper into Mastery... Don't miss out!

Chapter 2
Issues of Taxation and Legal Formalities

There are legal and tax consequences to consider when deciding on a company structure for a startup. In addition, a new firm must take a giant leap forward while deciding on a corporate structure. Consequences include changes to fixed expenses, legal exposure, and the composition of your company's support staff. Since your company's structure has immediate tax ramifications, it is important to consider this issue during this time of year.

2.1 Taxes and Other Legal Implications

Do not worry; we have laid out the most popular company structures and their tax implications for you below.

Business Structure Essentials

The concept of "business formation" refers to the way a business is organized and operated. Selecting an appropriate business formation is a crucial step in launching a business. While it might not directly influence the daily operations, it is instrumental in defining ownership, minimizing liability, optimizing tax management, and facilitating future expansion.

The Role of Business Entities

Business entities serve as the foundation, enabling your business to operate with its own identity, separate from your personal identity. They allow the business to have its own bank accounts, enter into contracts, and conduct transactions. For entrepreneurs aiming to transform their ventures into full-time occupations or those looking to enter into contracts or hire employees, establishing a formal business entity and registering it with the state is recommended.

Understanding Business Contracts

In the business world, contracts are commonplace. Individuals often find themselves entering into agreements, representing themselves. However, businesses, represented by their appointed officials, must adhere to legal and state regulations to validate contracts. Operating as a registered business entity ensures that personal assets remain protected in the event of business-related issues.

Liability and Business Types

By default, if you commence a business without official registration, you operate as a sole proprietor, meaning you are personally liable for any business-related issues. Establishing a Limited Liability Company (LLC), corporation, or partnership transfers this liability to the business entity, offering a layer of protection for personal assets.

Tax Considerations and Professional Assistance

As businesses grow and income streams stabilize, tax implications become a focal point. The costs associated with establishing and maintaining a business can be significant, varying by state. While entrepreneurs can navigate the registration process independently, many choose to enlist legal assistance to ensure compliance with all regulatory requirements. Consulting with tax profession-als is also advisable to align the business structure with long-term financial objectives, ensuring tax efficiency and compliance.

2.2 Business Structure Types

1. Sole proprietorship

The organization is run in the form of a single proprietorship. The Internal Revenue Service defines a single proprietor as a person who both owns and operates a business. The fundamen-tal benefit of a proprietorship is the ease with which it can be set up and run. There is no separation between the owner and the company under sole proprietorship, therefore the owner keeps all the money made. On the other hand, this status makes the proprietor liable for the company's debts, losses, and obliga-tions. As a result, owners' personal accounts and assets may be at risk if the company's financial resources are insufficient to pay out pending claims. Freelance work may be found in many fields, such as writing, consulting, tutoring, and catering.

Overview of liabilities

A company's liabilities are the costs and commitments it has incurred because of doing business.

When it comes to legal responsibility, limited liability guaran-tees that business partners or owners will never be held respon-sible for more than their initial investment. In terms of wheth-er a company with liability faces legal action the claimants can only sue the company itself and cannot touch the personal as-sets of investors or owners.

On the hand personal liability comes into play when business owners' assets can be used to cover any debts incurred by their business.

However, in corporations there is a concept called "piercing the
veil" which is commonly used to settle debts. This occurs when
serious misconduct takes place and courts disregard liability by
holding shareholders responsible for the actions or debts of the
corporation.

Pass-Through Entity Explained

In the realm of federal income taxation, a sole proprietorship is
often classified as a "pass-through entity," meaning the business
itself isn't subject to income tax. Instead, the income "passes
through" to the owner, who reports it on their personal tax return and pays the appropriate income tax. This model simplifies
the tax process but places the tax burden squarely on the owner.

Sole Proprietorship: A Double-Edged Sword

While starting a sole proprietorship is cost-effective and free from
complex legal formalities, it comes with the drawback of personal
liability. The owner is directly responsible for all business debts
and legal issues. Moreover, the business income is subject to
self-employment tax, and the unregistered nature of the business
can sometimes impact its perceived professionalism.

Partnership: A Collaborative Venture

Partnerships involve two or more individuals sharing the responsibilities of business operations and liabilities. General
partnerships entail shared management duties and liabilities,
while limited partnerships include general and limited partners, with the latter having limited liability and no management

involvement. Limited liability partnerships offer liability protection for all partners, balancing responsibility and control.

Limited Liability Company (LLC): A Hybrid Model

LLCs blend features of corporations and partnerships, offering liability protection and tax flexibility. They can be classified differently for tax purposes, allowing owners to choose the most beneficial tax treatment. However, establishing and maintaining an LLC involves some complexities and costs.

Corporation: A Separate Legal Entity

Corporations operate as independent legal entities, offering liability protection for shareholders. C corporations are subject to double taxation, while S corporations allow income to pass through to shareholders, avoiding double taxation but with certain eligibility criteria. Corporations offer continuity and a structured management model but involve more complexities and costs in establishment and operation.

Weighing the Options

Each business structure comes with its unique set of advantages, liabilities, and tax implications. Choosing the right one involves considering factors like the level of liability protection needed, tax preferences, and the business's size and nature. It's essential to evaluate each option carefully to align with the business's goals and operational needs.

Business Structures and Their Tax Benefits and Detriments

BUSINESS STRUCTURES	TAX PROS	TAX CONS
Sole Proprietorship	Simple tax filing; income is reported on the owner's personal tax return.	Owner is subject to self-employment tax; no separate business tax benefits.
Partnership	Income is passed through to partners, who report it on their personal tax returns; potential for business expense deductions.	Partners are personally liable for business debts and liabilities; complex tax filing for multiple owners.
Limited Liability Company (LLC)	Offers choice in tax classification, allowing for flexibility; members are not personally liable for business debts.	Can be subject to self-employment tax; tax complexity increases with the number of members.
C Corporation	Income is taxed at the corporate rate, which can be lower; provides personal liability protection for shareholders.	Subject to double taxation - income is taxed at the corporate level and again on shareholders' personal returns when distributed as dividends.

S Corporation	Income passes through to shareholders, avoiding double taxation; provides liability protection.	Eligibility restrictions; shareholders must report income and losses on personal tax returns, potentially increasing their tax liability.

How to Decide on a Company Structure

Evaluating your business's future objectives, plans for expansion, and potential legal risks is essential in determining the appropriate business structure. While proprietorships can be suitable for smaller ventures or part-time businesses, formal registration with the state often provides enhanced benefits and protections.

LLCs are a popular choice for startups not seeking external funding, offering flexibility for single or multiple owners and less complexity than a full-scale corporation. Opting for S Corporation tax classification can be beneficial for LLC owners actively involved in the business, offering specific tax advantages.

For businesses aiming to attract external investors and potentially becoming publicly traded, a C Corporation is often the preferred structure. It accommodates an extensive shareholder base and provides a framework for public trading.

Investing in professional legal or tax advice to navigate the selection of a business structure can be a prudent expense, ensuring alignment with your specific needs and goals. This decision is pivotal, influencing factors from investor attraction to liability management and regulatory compliance.

The choice of a legal structure requires a thorough assessment of the business's current status and future aspirations. It's a decision intertwined with legal, operational, and financial implications. After settling on a structure, the focus shifts back to optimizing operational efficiency and boosting profitability.

2.3 Impact on Income and Profit Taxation

Deciding on the structure of your business can affect how much you will pay in income and profit taxes. The legal structure you choose will determine the tax obligations, who is responsible for paying taxes and the overall tax amount owed. It is crucial to grasp these tax implications before deciding as they can significantly impact your business well-being. Below is an explanation of how your choice of structure affects income and profit taxation.

Sole Proprietorship:

When it comes to income taxation, in a proprietorship the owner and the business are treated as one entity for tax purposes. This means that any profits or losses generated by the business are reported on the owner's tax return using Schedule C of Form 1040. All profits from the firm must be taxed at the owner's personal income tax rate.

Regarding profit taxation sole proprietors are not required to pay taxes for their business profits. Instead, the owner's personal income tax rate applies to these gains. This arrangement can be beneficial for businesses since it may result in lower tax rates.

Partnership:

Partnerships have a tax setup known as pass through taxation. This implies that the partnership does not pay taxes on the business's profits or losses. Instead, they "pass through" to the partners who report their portion of the income or losses, on their tax returns. Each partner is responsible for paying income tax on his or her proportionate share of the partnership's earnings.

Limited Liability Company (LLC):

Income Taxation: An LLC is a business structure that has the flexibility to choose its tax treatment. It functions as a partnership-style "pass-through" entity by default. However, a limited liability company may elect to be treated for tax purposes as either a subchapter S or a subchapter C corporation.

The income and losses of a limited liability company (LLC) are distributed to its members for tax purposes if the LLC is treated as a pass-through organization. These members then report these outcomes on their tax returns. If the LLC opts for taxation, it will be subject to income tax on its profits, at the tax rate.

C Corporation:

Income Taxation: C corporations are considered as entities, under the law. They must pay taxes on their earnings at the standard corporation rate. The stockholders of C corporation are shielded from personal liability for the obligations of the business. However, they may potentially face a situation where they are taxed twice when they receive dividends.

Profit Taxation: C corporations have the responsibility of filing their tax returns and paying income tax based on their profits. Shareholders, on the hand, are liable to be taxed on any dividends or capital gains they receive from the corporation. This aspect can sometimes lead to a scenario where double taxation occurs.

S Corporation:

When it comes to federal income taxation, S companies "pass through" businesses like partnerships & sole proprietorships. This means that they do not have to pay income tax at the level. Instead, shareholders are required to report their portion of the corporation's income or losses on their tax returns.

Profit Taxation: Like partnerships and sole proprietorships, S corporations follow a level of taxation. In this system the corporation itself is not liable for paying income tax. Instead, shareholders are liable for paying taxes on their portion of the company's income.

The choice of structure for your business can have an impact on how income and profits are taxed. It is crucial to consider factors like liability protection, ease of management and tax implications when making this decision. Seeking advice from a tax professional or attorney can assist you in navigating the intricacies of tax law and selecting the structure for your business while optimizing your tax situation. Moreover, it is important to stay updated on evolving tax laws and regulations and adjust your business structure accordingly to minimize taxes and maximize profits.

Chapter 3
Tax Registration and Initial Compliance

Navigating sales tax compliance can be a time-consuming task, in the United States. Each state has its sales tax authority that establishes regulations for businesses regarding tax collection. Because of the many revisions and ongoing updates to these requirements, keeping track of where and when you need to collect sales tax from customers may be difficult.

3.1 Steps for Tax Registration

This comprehensive guide aims to assist you in determining the steps for registering to collect tax in the US. By doing you can avoid penalties and interest associated with non-compliance. It will also help you determine how to register for sales tax in different states. Furthermore, if you must collect sales tax but have not registered yet, this guide will offer insights into what actions should be taken. Finally, we will examine how Stripe can simplify your tax compliance management.

When Should You Get a Tax ID Number?

Registration for sales tax is required in every state in the United States when your business meets the state's minimum size, revenue, or other criteria. For sellers outside of a state, the economic nexus is typically used to determine when registration and collection of sales taxes are required. The economic nexus thresholds are determined based on sales revenue, transaction volume or sometimes both. For instance, if you conduct business in California and your sales revenue from customers in California exceeds $500,000, you must. Collect sales tax. Conversely, in Georgia, once your sales revenue surpasses $100,000. You have completed two hundred transactions with customers; in Georgia, you must start collecting sales tax.

The steps to getting a US sales tax license.

Here are the broad strokes of registering to collect sales tax with a state:

1. First, compile all relevant company and contact data.

2. Visit the website of your state Department of Revenue.

3. Look for their website's "Sales and Use Tax" section to begin registering your business.

4. Remember that each state has its sales tax authority, so you must register in states where you meet the tax registration requirements. To get started, check out the state's tax agency online.

5. Keep in mind that some states are exempt from sales tax registration processes thanks to their participation in the Sales and Use Tax Agreement (SSUTA). This agreement was designed to simplify sales tax registration. Twenty-four states (Arkansas, Georgia, Rhode Island, Indiana, Iowa, Michigan, Minnesota, Nebraska, Kansas, Kentucky, Nevada, North Carolina, New Jersey, North Dakota, Oklahoma, Ohio, North Dakota, Tennessee, Utah, South Dakota, South Dakota, Wisconsin, West Virginia, Vermont, Washington, & Wyoming) have adopted SSUTA.

If you are a seller and want to register through the Sales Tax Registration System (SSTRS), please note that you still need to set up accounts with each participating state. Additionally, if you have sales tax obligations, separate registrations will be required in any SSUTA conforming state(s).

You have alternatives if you have previously fulfilled the tax registration criteria in a state but have yet to register. If it has been over a month since you went over the tax registration threshold, consulting sales tax specialists may help you figure out what to do next. Many states have disclosure programs that assist sellers in resolving any sales tax obligations. Additionally, you might qualify for a state's amnesty program, which can help you become compliant. Do not start levying taxes until registered with the appropriate government agency.

How Stripe can help

Determining your sales tax obligations and registration requirements can become complex due to the factors involved. If you adhere to the nexus standard, Stripe Tax helps in monitoring your obligations. It will notify you when you reach a sales tax registration threshold based on your transactions processed through Stripe.

Stripe Tax offers the following benefits.

1. Understanding where to register and collect taxes: You can easily identify the locations where tax collection is necessary by analyzing your Stripe transactions. Once registered, you can activate tax collection for a state or country within seconds. Integrating tax collection into your existing Stripe setup requires one line of code. You can enable it with a simple click for Stripes no-code products like Invoicing.
2. When you are eligible, Stripe Tax will direct you to the appropriate state tax agency's website, where you can fill out your registration.

3. Automated sales tax collection: Stripe Tax ensures the calculation and collection of the sales tax am regardless of what or where you are selling it. It stays updated with tax rules and rate changes supporting various products and services.

Make filing and remittance easier; Stripe provides reports and tax summaries for every location where you must file and pay taxes. This makes it simple for you to manage the tax process independently with the assistance of your accountant or by working alongside a Stripe filing partner.

3.2 Documents for Initial Compliance

Before starting your return, examine the tax preparation checklist below. If you and your spouse are filing a joint tax return, you will also need your partner's information.

Personal Information

The Internal Revenue Service (IRS) and state tax agencies utilize the information you provide to confirm your identity, get in touch, and decide where to send your tax refund. All you need to do is provide your name as it appears on your Social Security card, along with your date of birth, Social Security Number, postal code, and copies of your previous year's federal and state tax returns. Your refund will then be sent directly to your provided bank account.

Dependent Information

To claim a family member or friend as a dependent, you will require the information.

- All dependents' names, ages, and Social Security (or other tax identification) numbers. If you can access their Social Security cards, use that information instead.
- Additionally, if the parent who has custody of your child is relinquishing their dependency exemption, you can do the same.

Sources of Income

Some documents can serve as proof of your earnings in 2022. Examples include:

- W-2 Employment Certifications
- Form 1099 G, which shows refunds of state and local taxes paid to you or your beneficiary.
- Statements of Interest (Form 1099 INT), Dividends (Form 1099 DIV), and Stock Purchases (Form 1099 B)
- Form 1099 R for retirement fund recipients and SSA 1099 for social security fund recipients
- If you sold a home or other property, the proceeds will be reported on Form 1099 S. Rental income will be reported on Form 1099 MISC.
- You will get a 1099 Q if you withdraw money from a 529 plan or a Coverdell education savings account.
- Health Savings Account distributions will be documented on Form 1099 SA.
- If your divorce or separation was finalized before the end of the year, any alimony payments you received should be included.
- Schedule K 1 reports earnings from pass-through companies, trusts or estates.
- Make sure to provide documentation for all cryptocurrency-related transactions.
- Include details about windfalls, like lottery prizes, jury duty pays, debt forgiveness, etc.

Self-Employment & Business Records

You should report any income you earn from your business. You may reduce your taxable income even more by deducting business-related costs.

- When reporting your earnings, use tax forms 1099 NEC and 1099 K if you are a contractor. It is crucial to maintain complete records.
- For home office costs, keep records of the footage of your house and the specific area dedicated to your workspace at home. Additionally, document the cost and date of installation for any assets owned by your company.
- Lastly, remember to keep track of transportation costs in terms of miles travelled.

Deductions

You might be able to reduce your tax payments or receive a refund by utilizing deductions. There are two options from which you can choose. You may either itemize your deductions or use the standard deductions, which are fixed dollar amounts depending on your filing status. You will need to provide the following details to itemize your deductions.

- Health care cost contributions
- Long-term care insurance premiums
- Mortgage interest Private Mortgage Insurance (PMI) and points paid over the tax year (these will be reported on Form 1098)
- Taxes on real estate
- State and local levies
- Costs associated with registering a vehicle.
- Donations made to profit organizations.
- Proof of damage incurred (if you resided in or owned property in an area designated as a federal disaster zone).

You do not need to list each deduction to benefit from any changes in income that follow.

- Form 1098 E, Interest in Student Loans Paid.
- Information about contributions to a health savings account, individual retirement account or self-employed 401(k).
- If your separation or divorce agreement is completed by December 31, you must pay alimony.
- Teachers receive reimbursement for the expenses incurred on materials.
- Costs incurred by sole proprietors for medical coverage.

Tax Credits

When you receive a tax credit, your overall tax liability is reduced by one dollar. You will need the following items to apply for tax credits:

1. Form 1098 T: The Higher Education Tax Statement provides information about your expenses.
2. Details about your childcare provider: Include their name, address, Social Security number and the amount you paid for childcare.
3. Adoption-related expenses: If you had adoption proceedings in 2022, provide the adoption fee and the child's Social Security number.
4. IRS Form 1095 A is necessary if you obtain health insurance through the Health Insurance Marketplace.

Gathering these documents will aid in claiming tax credits during your filing process.

Estimated Tax Payments

If you work for yourself or receive an amount of income without any taxes being deducted, you might need to make estimated tax payments. It is important not to pay taxes, so include these estimated amounts when filing your tax return. The payments are typically made annually to the Internal Revenue Service and state or local governments as estimates. Additionally, any refunds for years can be carried over. Applied to the current year's taxes. Remember to consider any payments made in conjunction with a delay.

Proof of Losses

You may be eligible to claim deductions for setbacks. If any of the following situations apply to you in 2022, please ensure you have evidence of your losses.

Remember to keep receipts and other documents that show the date and original amount paid for any stocks or other investments where you expect to claim a loss.

Keep accurate records of all your debts, whether business or personal. For example, if you lent money to a friend and they never paid it back, that would be considered a debt.

Although gathering this information before filing your tax return requires some effort, it ensures that you take advantage of every tax deduction and credit.

After filing your return, storing your tax paperwork securely in case of audits is important. The IRS or state tax authorities may request proof of income and deductions if they review your return. Having all this information organized together will help expedite the process and prevent any loss of deductions or credits.

3.3 Ongoing Tax Deadlines and Compliance

Are you a citizen of the United States or a Green Card Holder living in Canada? Are you interested in U.S. Or foreign business entities? Are you an individual or business owner interested in the U.S.? Or you are responsible for ensuring your business is tax-compliant? You need to know the dates and deadlines for filing your income tax.

Tax filing deadlines in your situation. For instance, if you are a U.S. Expat residing in Canada, the deadline for filing your U.S. Income tax return with the Internal Revenue Service (IRS) is April 15 (April 18, 2023). However, individuals who are U.S. Citizens or residents and have their home and abode outside of the United States and Puerto Rico are granted an extension until June 15.

To request extensions, you can act by filing Form 4868. This form grants an extension allowing you to extend the filing deadline until October 15 (October 16, 2023). Alternatively, you can send a letter to the IRS explaining your situation and seeking their approval for an extension. You will have until December 15 to submit your tax return if accepted. For U.S. Expats who need time to meet Foreign Earned Income Exclusion (FEIE) requirements, a special extension is available by filing Form 2350. It allows for a deadline specifically tailored to meet FEIE requirements.

Taxpayers must consult with a US tax advisor or professional to determine whether they need to file a tax return or form, which specific form is required, and the applicable due date based on their circumstances. It is important to note that there may be exceptions and variations in the information provided here. This data is meant to provide context. It is not intended to serve as legal or tax advice. Additionally, it covers used forms. It may not include every form or due date that could apply in individual cases. Therefore, reviewing your U.S. Tax filing requirements with a U.S. Tax advisor is advisable.

An extension request does not provide you with further time to pay taxes. To avoid any overdue payment penalties or interest charges, it is important to either pay your taxes when you file for an extension or submit your tax return on time with the payment.

Please note that dates for filing taxes and forms are adjusted and revised each year. The due dates provided below are specifically for filing tax returns or forms in 2023 applicable to the 2022 tax year (assuming you follow the calendar year; if your fiscal year end is different, it is best to consult with a U.S. Tax advisor).

This information is solely meant for purposes. For determining the tax filing date based on your unique circumstances, please contact a qualified U.S. Tax advisor.

Chapter 4
Income and Expense Management

4.1 Importance of Accurate Records

Every individual involved in business needs to maintain documentation. The maintenance of records holds significance for the success of your business. Maintaining records will assist you in ways.

- Tracking how your company is doing as time goes on.
- Preparing comprehensive financial statements
- Identifying the various sources contributing to your income
- Tracking deductible expenses effectively
- Keeping a record of your property basis value
- Facilitating the preparation of your tax returns
- Providing support for items reported on your tax returns.

Tracking how your company is doing as time goes on.

Keeping records is essential for monitoring the growth of your business. These records can provide insights into improving your business, identify top-selling items and highlight areas where adjustments may be necessary. Maintaining records significantly enhances the chances of achieving success in your business endeavors.

Preparing comprehensive financial statements

To ensure the accuracy of statements, it is essential to maintain records. These records encompass income statements (profit and loss) as balance sheets. Such statements are invaluable when dealing with institutions or creditors and play a role in effectively managing your business.

An income statement summarizes a company's earnings and expenditure over time.

A balance sheet, on the other hand, is a snapshot of a business's assets, liabilities, and equity as of a certain date.

Identifying the various sources contributing to your income

You may receive money or assets from sources. Documenting the sources of one's financial support is crucial. This information will assist you in distinguishing between business and non-earnings, as well as taxable and non-taxable income.

Tracking deductible expenses effectively

If you do not keep a record of your expenses when they happen, you might forget to include them when preparing your tax return.

Documenting the original purchase price of a piece of property

For income tax purposes, your basis is your property investment's value. It calculates the profit or loss when you sell, exchange, or dispose of the property as deductions for depreciation, amortization, depletion, and casualty losses.

Facilitating the preparation of your tax returns

To ensure tax returns, it is essential to maintain records. These records should provide evidence of the income, expenses, and credits you declare. Typically, the same set of records you use to track your business and create statements can be utilized.

Providing evidence for goods included in tax returns.

It is important to have your business records easily accessible for IRS inspections. If the IRS decides to review any of your tax returns, you may need to clarify the reported items. Having a collection of records will expedite the examination process.

4.2 Personal Vs. Business Finances

There are commonalities and distinctions between financial plans for individuals and businesses. Budgeting, taxation, investment, and the formulation of long-term objectives are all shared practices. While discussing the similarities between these two essential planning practices is vital, it is also critical to emphasize how they vary. As a business owner, it is in your best interest to do some financial planning for yourself and your company. Now, let us look at some of the most vital factors.

In most cases, it is more difficult to plan a company's finances than an individual. When preparing for a business, you need to think about things like payroll and inventory management that are not as important when planning for yourself or your family.

We would be negligent if we did not stress the significance of classifying your company and personal funds from the start. Confusing the two, even unintentionally, may cause serious problems with filing taxes, making large purchases, and even considering mergers and acquisitions.

Simplicity & Complexity

When it comes to managing finances, it is important to invest an amount of time. On the other hand, business planning calls for a more meticulous approach. This is because it is a process. Business budgets are more complex than simple lists of costs since they take into consideration things like accounting, risk management, predictions, and individual department allocations. Neglecting planning for your business can have long-lasting consequences.

Moreover, it is worth noting that financial planning can be overwhelming and confusing. Based on our discussions with business leaders across industries, one key takeaway is the importance of establishing a set of practices and utilizing frameworks to simplify this complexity. This may involve leveraging technology or resources within your bank's portal or implementing frameworks like Profit First and EOS (Entrepreneur Operating System) to convert goals into manageable weekly routines that contribute towards achieving those objectives.

Regardless of the tools and frameworks you choose for planning purposes, having the team in place is crucial for executing these essential functions.

Taxes

When it comes to taxes, both individuals and businesses have an obligation. However, when considering taxes, it is important to remember that filing your income tax is the tax you need to focus on. As a business owner, though, you are planning, and tax preparation must adhere to the laws and regulations set by local, regional, and federal authorities. Here are three key areas that distinguish business taxes from taxes.

Income Tax

The funds allocated for your business earnings in a given calendar year.

Employment Tax

The sum is set aside for your staff's share of Medicare and Social Security taxes.

Excise Tax

The fees imposed on goods, services, and activities. The fees you incur depend on the kind of company you offer and the items you offer. A tax expert should be consulted early in the planning process.

For every business we engage with in Central Indiana and beyond, the key is to plan, prepare and organize today to achieve success tomorrow. By doing you can ensure a stress-free tax season for yourself and your team. Moreover, this approach will enable you to assess the growth of your business.

Multiple Income Stream

There are several potential revenue streams for your firm to explore. It is an approach to have sources of income by offering assorted products and services rather than relying solely on one core offering. Whether it is income, monthly subscriptions, rental earnings, one-time services, investments, or ongoing commitments, it is important to monitor and plan your financial goals based on your diverse income streams.

On the other hand, when it comes to income streams, for individuals, the tracking, planning, and forecasting processes are often not as strictly regulated in many cases.

Investments

Investments play a role in business and financial planning, but it is essential to recognize their subtle differences. Expenses are unavoidable in both realms, whether running a business or managing finances. On the other hand, businesses would do well to see costs as opportunities to put money into profitable ventures.

Leveraging one's assets may be beneficial for company owners when making investments. To leverage is to borrow money to undertake an investment that might provide a profit. It can also refer to taking on debt to finance business assets. The smart use of leverage can significantly enhance a business's purchasing power. Help the little guys and gals trying to make it big.

From a banking perspective, it is important to consider two elements of leverage: debt and equity. Having a low debt-to-equity ratio is a positive sign for any company. This deliberate financial planning approach enables relationship managers at your banking institution to facilitate access to much-needed capital.

4.3 Cash Flow Management

Managing cash flow is crucial for businesses as it helps determine the money needed to cover obligations, such as paying employees and suppliers. The primary goal of cash flow management is to ensure that there is money to manage expenses and debts and provide for the business itself. It is not uncommon for businesses to face cash flow shortages at some point, which can hinder their ability to meet their commitments. By managing cash flow, these challenges can be minimized. Businesses generate cash through three avenues: selling products and services (cash from operations), obtaining loans, or selling shares (cash from finance), and selling assets (cash from investing). The cash flow management process revolves around securing a sustainable inflow of cash from these sources.

Tracking Business Cash Flow

Tools are used in business to monitor cash flow.

1. Cash flow projection helps businesses anticipate their cash availability by plotting expected income and expenses on a calendar.
2. Cash flow statements provide insights into how much cash is generated from operations (sales) compared to funds obtained through loans or the selling of assets.

Budgeting and financial planning for lean times

When businesses face the possibility of strain, they can adapt their approach to managing outgoing funds.

Managing inflows

Improving cash flow reliability; invoice processing. Shorten the payment window for customers. Act on payments. Provide payment options such as card payments or direct debit. Consider retaining customers on service contracts.

Boosting cash inflows: For businesses experiencing recurring cash flow challenges, it may be necessary to reassess pricing strategies to ensure profit margins.

Exploring financing options: Loans can offer a lifeline for businesses during periods. Some seasonal enterprises even rely on financing solutions to navigate through the year.

Managing outflows

To make cash outflows more manageable and easier to predict, consider postponing expenses to align with periods of cash flow. Explore the possibility of negotiating instalment payments with suppliers or making lump sum payments. Additionally, leasing equipment or resources could be an alternative to purchasing them.

To reduce cash outflows, Businesses have the potential to reduce essential spending by comparing prices for supplies from various sources and consider exploring opportunities for bulk purchasing agreements.

Chapter 5
Tax Deductions for Small Businesses

Companies pay costs like rent, equipment, and payroll, which enable employees to make products and services that generate revenue. While a company's accounting team can deduct some of these expenses for tax purposes, other expenses are nondeductible. If you are pursuing a career in finance or management, learning about the diverse types of expenses you might encounter in a small business can help you create accurate budgets and tax reports.

5.1 Types of Deductible Expenses

Here is additional information regarding twenty business expenses encompassing both nondeductible costs.

1. Advertising

Advertising costs refer to the expenses a company bears to attract a customer's attention to the business or its products. This may include expenses related to advertising in media outlets and costs associated with email marketing. Additionally, it encompasses expenses for items like brochures, website design, business cards and branded promotional items. Typically, these expenses are eligible for deduction.

2. Meals & entertainment

Employer-provided meals and entertainment may qualify as a deductible business cost. Business entertainment might include planning office parties for the holidays or buying concert tickets for the workforce. Exceptions include meals served at private parties.

3. Utilities, rent & phone

Rent or lease payments a company makes, as expenses related to phones and utilities, fall under this category. Additional utility costs encompass electricity, water, garbage collection, heating, and security charges. These expenses can be claimed as deductions.

4. Travel

When employees go on business trips or attend events that can be advantageous, you can categorize these expenses under travel to the company. This category encompasses any travel that takes employees away from their workplace for enough time to necessitate sleep or rest. Eligible expenses include transportation fares, flight tickets, accommodation fees, dry cleaning charges, long-distance phone calls, meals, and gratuities.

5. Payroll & employee benefits

Most of a company's payroll costs are allowed to be written off. Employee rewards include any monetary or non-monetary incentives provided to workers by an employer to retain them. For example, you can include retirement benefits, paid vacation, group insurance, health, disability, life or dental, and training.

6. Transportation

Business transportation expenses refer to the costs associated with commuting to a workplace. It is important to note that this deduction does not cover transportation from home to the company's building. These expenses encompass vehicle costs or mileage. The IRS offers guidelines to help you calculate the amount per mile.

7. Office expenses

The category of office expenses encompasses the costs incurred by a business for equipment, furniture and supplies that are essential for its operations. This includes items such as software, printers, and computers. Office supplies also fall under this category. Include provisions like water, coffee, food meant for clients, and cleaning supplies.

8. Depreciation section

Certain possessions owned by a company have the potential to decrease in value or depreciate as time goes on. The accountants of these companies typically document this depreciation to monitor the decline in the value of their assets. As an illustration, let us consider the equipment a manufacturing company owns, which will lose value each year. This depreciation amount can be claimed as an expense.

9. Professional services

Many small businesses hire professionals for support, accounting, and other professional services. The expenses incurred for these services, such as costs or payments made to consultants and external accountants, fall under the category of professional services expenses. This category enables businesses to deduct the costs associated with hiring consultants since they could have deducted wages if they had employed them directly.

10. Interest expenses

Deducting interest payments on mortgages and business loans is a business expense category. Additionally, you can deduct bank fees and loan origination fees. Check printing fees. This deduction can be particularly helpful for businesses that have taken out startup loans.

5.2 Rules and Limitations

Small business owners understand the burden of taxes. However, you may keep more of your hard-earned cash by taking advantage of tax deductions. Deductions are available to you no matter what kind of company you run or your sector. A new computer or mobile phone bill may be deducted from your taxable income, which may surprise some. To make the most of these opportunities during the 2023 tax season, consult our checklist to identify which business tax deductions you qualify for.

1. Home office

Remote and combined office environments have become more common in recent years. You may deduct the cost per square foot of your home office if you use it for business.

Per the guidelines provided by the IRS, individuals who work from home can claim a deduction of $5 for every foot of space utilized as a home office with a limit of three hundred square feet. This means that the maximum deduction one can claim is $1,500.

Utilities (including gas, electric and Wi-Fi) are included in the home office deduction and cannot be claimed separately.

In 2022, there will be three criteria that must be met to claim a home office deduction.

1. The workspace should have clearly defined boundaries. It should ideally be a room or section within a room. The deduction does not apply if you are working from your bedroom.
2. The workspace must be your primary place of work. You may not qualify for this deduction if you primarily work in a working space but occasionally use your kitchen table for work purposes.
3. You must conduct significant business activities from your home office.

For instance, if you work as a healthcare in a hospital and conduct tasks and manage financial matters from the comfort of your home, it is unlikely that you would meet the criteria.

2. Office supplies

Whether you are working remotely or in an office setting, items are necessary to keep your business operations running smoothly. That is why the Internal Revenue Service lets companies write off some of their office supply costs. Printer paper, markers, pencils, other writing instruments, and essential computer software for your company are all examples of supplies for the workplace that qualify as business costs.

3. Business insurance premiums

It is crucial to have insurance for your business to ensure its financial well-being. Certain types of business insurance are necessary if you plan on leasing office space or obtaining a business license. The good news is that insurance premiums paid on behalf of a company qualify for a tax write-off. In most cases, premiums paid for products, including general liability, professional liability, commercial property, business interruption, and cyber insurance, may be deducted from taxable income. Employee insurance includes medical, disability, uninsured motorist, and death benefits.

4. Office rent

Small business owners who lease office space can deduct their rental expenses from their income. This deduction includes the cost of renting the building and covers the expenses incurred for a business parking garage.

This deduction for a rented property is distinct from the home office deduction. The latter applies to business owners renting space outside their residential premises.

If you happen to rent your home or apartment and work, from there time, it is advisable to claim the home office deduction.

5. Relocation expenses

Twenty-seven million Americans relocated in the year 2022. Whether it was a move within their state or across the country, individuals who moved their businesses can potentially recover some or all the associated expenses.

When deducting relocation costs for 2022, eligibility depends on the type of small business one owns. Moving expenses may be deducted from corporate taxes for businesses organized as corporations or limited liability companies. This category includes shipping, packaging, loading, surveying, and brokerage fees. On the other hand, if you run your business as a proprietorship or partnership, you may be eligible for deduction if two conditions are met: firstly, you must relocate at least 50 miles away from your previous location; secondly, within 12 months following your relocation, you must have worked at least 39 weeks at the new location.

But keep in mind that home offices are not eligible for this deduction. Therefore, claiming this tax credit would be impossible if you operate your business from home and decide to move into a house for any reason.

6. Internet & phone bills

You can claim a deduction for the expenses of your internet and cellphone plan on your income taxes for 2022 as per the IRS guidelines. The condition is that your business heavily relies on phone and internet usage for day-to-day operations.

Wi-Fi costs used for business while travelling or staying in a hotel may also be deducted from your taxable income.

However, things grow more complicated when you use your business phone and internet for personal reasons. The IRS states that you can deduct the proportion of expenses related to conducting your business.

7. Business vehicles

Business vehicles can be claimed as a tax deduction. However, if you also use your business vehicle for purposes, calculating the deduction can become a bit tricky.

For example, self-employed individuals who use their cars for business reasons might be interested in deducting expenses from their hired and nonowner auto insurance policy (HNOA). In this case, the percentage of time the vehicle is used for business activities is what the deduction should be predicated on. Keep track of each trip you make for business and use that mileage cost as your deduction. The mileage rate may also be used, with the rates being $0.585/mile from January 1, 2022, through June 30, 2022, and $0.625/mile from July 1, 2022, through December 31, 2022.

If the vehicle is exclusively used for business purposes and never used for travel (such as a work van), you can deduct the cost of operating and maintaining it.

You may deduct any cost associated with your automobile, including.

- Maintenance & repairs
- Gas
- Car insurance
- Lease payments
- Registration fees
- Parking fees
- Tolls
- License fees

8. Employee salaries & benefits

One of the tax deductions available to small business owners is the expense associated with paying employee salaries and providing employee benefits. This deduction, however, is only available if you have other workers than yourself. It does not apply to proprietors, partners, or members of an LLC.

Paid time off, commissions, and bonuses may all be deducted from an employee's taxable income and base salary. Furthermore, employment taxes related to payroll are also eligible for deduction.

9. Business credit card & loan interest

The interest you pay on company loans or credit cards is tax deductible. However, there are rules set by the IRS for business owners who wish to claim this deduction.

1. You must have liability for the debt.
2. Both you and your lender should expect the debt to be repaid.
3. You and the lender should have a debtor-creditor relationship.

For 2022, the maximum allowable interest deduction is 30% of taxable income.

10. Independent contractors

Are you utilizing the services of contractors or freelancers for your business? If so, you may write off their fees as a business expense. However, there is a rule to keep in mind for this deduction.

1. The contractor should not be considered an employee of your business.

2. The services provided must be for your business and not for use as the owner.

If you make payments to independent contractors or freelancers of $600 or more in a given tax year, you must issue them a Form 1099 NEC. Failure to provide this form to a contractor could result in penalties if audited.

11. Startup business expenses

Do you hope to launch a company in 2022? You will be glad to know that the IRS allows entrepreneurs like yourself to deduct 100% of their startup expenses with a limit of $5,000.

To be eligible for this deduction, the expense should be something that an established business would normally deduct. In this context, it means money spent before your company opens its doors for business.

There are types of startup expenses that could potentially qualify for this deduction. Some examples include working alongside a business consultant, attending conferences in your industry, participating in training events, to your field launching marketing campaigns, and even building a website.

12. Business losses

If your business incurred a loss in the year, the IRS permits you to deduct the loss. Sole proprietors and LLC owners can fully deduct these losses from their tax returns. Your ability to write off an unlimited sum of money is guaranteed. Furthermore, consecutive years of business losses will not result in any penalties being imposed.

13. Legal & professional fees

Collaborating with professionals, like lawyers, accountants, or bookkeepers, can be considered a business tax write-off. If the services these professionals provide are necessary and relevant to your business, you can deduct them from your taxes.

14. Charitable contributions

In 2022, businesses displayed a deal of generosity on both global scales. Numerous headlines highlighted their acts of giving to those in need. If your business donated to an organization in the taxable year, you could reduce your tax liability by utilizing it.

Donations given in cash to a qualified charity are tax deductible at 60% for the current tax year. The IRS suggests reporting charitable gifts on personal taxes if your firm is a sole proprietorship or an LLC. Nonetheless, if your company is an S corporation, you should itemize deductions on your corporate tax return.

5.3 Maximizing Deduction Opportunities

To what extent should one make use of tax advantages and deductions? Maximizing deductions and credits involves utilizing all the tax deductions and credits to lower your income. This can potentially reduce your tax liability. Increase your tax refund. Knowing the difference between the two is crucial. A tax credit decreases your tax liability, while a tax deduction lowers your take-home pay. Depending on your line of business, you may be eligible to deduct things like real estate expenses and freelancer fees.

As a result of missing potential tax breaks, many owners of small businesses wind up owing money to the government. Seeking assistance ensures that your small business taxes are accurately filed to maximize deductions and credits. Keep reading as we explore seven strategies for saving money on taxes that can benefit your business this tax season.

Examples of Tax Deductions

As mentioned previously, a tax deduction is utilized to lower your income, resulting in paying taxes on a reduced amount. Here are a few instances of tax deductions.

Health insurance: Freelancers with healthcare plans can deduct this expense from their tax filings.

Property taxes: This deduction applies to individuals who own rental property since it is considered a business expenditure.

Travel expenses: Self-employed truck drivers often can deduct the costs of lodging and meals while travelling for work.

Examples of Tax Credits

A tax credit can have two effects it can. Cut your tax bill in half or get a bigger refund. Individual tax credits may be one of two types.

1. The Earned Income Tax Credit (EITC) is a known tax credit for individuals with a moderate-income level.
2. The Plug-in Electric Drive Vehicle Credit: If you qualify and have bought a vehicle (EV) after August 16, 2022, you might be eligible for this credit.

5.4 Maximizing Your Deductions & Credits

To ensure you take advantage of tax deductions and credits you qualify for, it is important to conduct research and plan. Incorporating your tax considerations into your bookkeeping practices is an approach. By maintaining small business bookkeeping records, you will simplify the tax season process. Maximize your deductions.

Start by creating a running list of your deductions throughout the year, then wait until the end of each quarter or month to record business expenses. Recording expenses immediately will save you time and effort. Additionally, remember to keep track of all your receipts. These practices help with your record keeping and prove invaluable in case of an audit by the IRS.

Understanding tax deductions and credits can be complex due to the print involved. It is best to collaborate with an expert who can make sure no essential elements are missed.

1. Make 401(k) & HSA Contributions

It is important to understand the significance of retirement savings regardless of age. This practice has two benefits: increasing tax savings and maximizing tax deductions. However, it is worth noting that the Internal Revenue Service (IRS) limits the retirement contributions you can deduct from your taxes. If possible, try to contribute the amount to maximize these benefits.

Your income level and 401(k) status will determine the limits for deducting contributions to Individual Retirement Accounts (IRAs). Make as much contribution as you can to your employer-sponsored retirement plan.

A Roth IRA is an alternative to a 401(k) since it may be funded using after-tax earnings. Roth Individual Retirement Account (IRA) contributions cannot be deducted from taxable income.

Some individuals may consider contributing to a Health Savings Account (HSA), which can be deducted from their taxes. According to the IRS, these contributions are tax-free if used for expenses. For 2022, individuals can deduct up to $3,650 and families up to $7,300, as stated in form Rev. Proc. 2021 25.

2. Make Charitable Donations

Donating to a cause gives you the satisfaction of supporting something meaningful and can also have financial benefits during tax season. Some charitable organizations may provide a statement for donors, but it is wise to keep track of your contributions as well.

Remember to itemize your deductions if you intend to reduce your adjusted income through donations. Opting for the deduction will not impact your tax return when claiming contributions.

Sometimes, deductions are limited to 50% of your adjusted income and should be directed towards qualified organizations. It is worth noting that this deduction becomes more advantageous if you make contributions, but consulting with a tax professional is always advisable for confirmation.

3. Postpone Your Income

Tax obligations are tied to the calendar year. Any expenses you claim as deductions must occur within that tax year. You cannot deduct an expense you plan to pay in 2023 of time. It is also worth noting that you may defer taxation on income until you get it.

People in this scenario might postpone receiving pay until next year. Some people may choose this option if their income varies significantly each year.

By paying taxes when you physically receive your income, you can postpone your end-of-year payments until after December 31, 2022. You must account for this delayed income when you file your tax return in 2023.

It is crucial to understand that deferring income does not exempt you from paying taxes on that amount; rather, it allows for a reduction in tax payments for the year. This can have an impact, especially if your income falls near the threshold of a tax bracket.

4. Pay for the Business Expenses Early

Like your earnings deductions, business taxes are claimed in the year you incur them. Just as you can delay receiving your income until the year, you can optimize your deductions by paying business expenses.

It is important for small business owners to always be aware of business expenses as they can offer tax advantages when they align with higher income.

Consider any last-minute business expenses that may need to be incurred before the end of the year. These expenses will still be counted towards 2022 even if you do not receive the goods or services until the year.

5. Consider the Losing Investments

Although reflecting on an investment that did not turn out as expected may not be pleasant, there might be a lining. You could leverage that loss to your advantage by lowering your adjusted income. Selling an investment at a loss can be seen as income, effectively reducing the amount of income you must report. Remember that there is a limit to how much you can claim in capital losses—up to $3,000—and any excess can be carried forward to offset gains.

Chapter 6
Payroll Taxes and Retirement Contributions

Hiring employees is an achievement for small business owners who have finally realized their dreams. However, as success and growth come hand in hand, they also bring along hurdles, such as dealing with payroll taxes. Employers who are not adequately prepared for this responsibility or lack accounting expertise may soon find they need help from a payroll service provider to ensure their stability.

6.1 Payroll Taxes

Payroll taxes are in place to support government assistance programs like Medicare, Social Security, and unemployment benefits. Typically, both employers and employees contribute to these taxes. There are instances where the sole responsibility lies with the employer.

Taxable employee

Taxable employees need to pay income tax and payroll taxes on their wages. When deciding whether an individual is an employee or an independent contractor, businesses might follow the IRS's common law guidelines.

How much tax do businesses have to pay?

Small business owners are responsible for fulfilling all the tax obligations imposed by the government well as those imposed by state and local governments where they hire employees. Employers should seek guidance from a certified tax expert if they have any uncertainties regarding their tax liabilities.

6.2 Payroll Tax Types of Small Business

Employers have payroll taxes to consider. Remember that these levies represent a percentage of a worker's salary. Here are some of the ones.

1. FICA is a two-part tax that covers Social Security and Medicare. The current rate is 15.3% of an employee's earnings, with 12.4% for Social Security and 2.9% for Medicare. The employer and employee share the tax liability equally, contributing 7.65% for FICA. It is worth noting that Social Security has a wage base limit of $160,200 for the year, meaning employees will no longer pay this tax after earning that amount. However, there is no cap for Medicare.
2. Individuals with incomes may need to pay an extra 0.9% towards Medicare. This applies to individuals earning $200,000 per year, couples filing jointly with an income of $250,000 per year and married couples filing separately with an income of $125,000 per year. Employers are required to deduct the Additional Medicare Tax from employees' wages but do not have to match it.
3. Under the Federal Unemployment Tax Act (FUTA), small businesses are typically liable for taxes if they pay their employees $1,500 or more in any given quarter or have at least one employee working part-time for 20 or more weeks. The

tax rate is 6% on the annual $7,000 an employee earns. Employers solely bear it.

4. Meanwhile, each state's State Unemployment Tax Act (SUTA) programs have variable tax rates. The good news is that if employers fulfil their SUTA obligations on time and do not fall under credit reduction states, they may qualify for a tax credit of 5.4%. This effectively reduces their FUTA rate to 0.6%. Like FUTA, SUTA taxes only apply to employers except in states where employees also contribute.

In addition to these state-level unemployment taxes, businesses may be required to pay payroll taxes depending on their location. These additional taxes might include payments towards short-term disability benefits, paid family leave and other assistance programs. Employers should consult with their government authorities or licensed tax professionals to stay updated on the rates and eligibility criteria.

Calculating payroll taxes for small businesses

When it comes to calculating business payroll taxes, there are a couple of factors to consider in addition to applying the appropriate rates.

1. Determining who is subject to the taxes.

Employers are obligated to pay payroll taxes for their employees, not contractors. An employee is someone whose work, including what tasks are performed and how they are conducted, is controlled by the person or entity paying for their services. Other financial considerations and the nature of the working relationship should also be considered.

2. Verifying wages.

Certain employee earnings, such as business expense reimbursements, non-monetary holiday gifts and cash advances, may not be subject to taxation. Before deducting taxes from an employee's wages, employers should also consider tax contributions towards benefits packages and whether the employee has reached any wage base limits (e.g., Social Security or FUTA).

These two aspects play a role in calculating small business payroll taxes.

Withholding small business payroll taxes

Employers deduct FICA taxes. Payroll deductions for SUTA taxes in states. Payroll processing comprises tallying employee compensation and deducting taxes at the proper rates. For instance, if employees earn $550 for a specific pay period, their Medicare tax contribution would be $7.98 (calculated as $550 multiplied by 1.45%).

Report & Pay Payroll Taxes

After employers have deducted the required payroll taxes from their employee's wages, they typically can submit the payments along with their tax liability to the IRS using the Electronic Federal Tax Payment System (EFTPS). Additionally, they must report the taxes deposited using the forms based on their specific business type. Some examples include the Annual Federal Tax Return (Form 944) filed by businesses, the Annual Federal Tax Return (Form 943) filed by agricultural employers, and the Annual Federal Unemployment (FUTA) Tax Return (Form 940) filed by businesses each year.

It is important to note that each location has its process for paying and reporting state payroll taxes.

Payroll tax deadlines & schedules

Typically, federal payroll taxes can be paid either on a basis or weekly basis depending on the amount of tax liability that an employer has reported in a previous timeframe or lookback period. When paying monthly, the deadline is the 15th of the month. However, weekly payments depend on the employer's payroll schedule. Taxes are payable the following Wednesday if the pay period finishes on a Wednesday, Thursday, or Friday. Taxes are payable the following Friday unless the pay period finishes on a Saturday, Sunday, Monday, or Tuesday.

What are the consequences of late or nonpayment of payroll taxes?

In their stages and facing financial challenges, numerous small businesses may find it difficult to meet their tax obligations. In some cases, the IRS imposes penalties that become more severe as the number of days of delay increases. Additionally, employers could face criminal consequences if the IRS determines they intentionally neglected their tax responsibilities.

ADP offers a range of affordable solutions to assist businesses with their payroll taxes. We have successfully assisted 800,000 businesses in improving their payroll processes. Most of our clients, two-thirds, have said that they now find it easier to comply with payroll taxes and regulations compared to when they were using another service provider.

Chapter 7

Sales Tax Management and Use Taxes

As a shopper, you are aware that sales tax is something you encounter when buying goods from retailers (unless you reside in one of the five states that do not impose a sales tax). The buyer is responsible for paying the sales tax to the retailer. Then forwards it to the state.

7.1 Collecting Sales Tax

You are the seller since you are the company owner. As a result, if your company has a physical location in more than one state, you must collect, record, and remit sales tax on all transactions made to residents of those states. This includes states where your building is located, where your employees reside or work or where your inventory is stored.

It is worth noting that each state sets its sales tax rates and regulations, which can be as diverse as comparing Minnesota weather to California. Local governments and counties may further complicate matters by adding their sales taxes.

Doing paperwork

You must obtain a license or a seller's permit from your state to collect sales tax. This license will assign you an identification number. You must maintain accurate records of all sales made by your business. Income tax receipts. At intervals (quarterly or annually), depending on the total value of your sales, you will need to file a return and make tax payments to the state.

Internet sales

The rise of Internet sales has brought about complexity. There is some debate over whether internet retailers should be required to collect sales tax from customers in jurisdictions where they do not physically operate. Certain states have implemented laws mandating the collection of sales taxes irrespective of presence. Moreover, the federal government is contemplating legislation that would impact this matter on a scale. If you wish to explore how this could potentially affect your business, I recommend searching for "[YourState] Internet sales tax."

7.2 Managing Sales Tax

Sales tax can be quite intricate for businesses regardless of their size. If your business has customers in states, the complexity and risk associated with sales tax increase accordingly. It starts with determining whether you have a connection (nexus) in a state or locality. Nowadays, nexus is primarily determined by two factors: presence or economic presence. Once nexus is established, determine if your products or services are subject to taxation. Registration and compliance with the rules are usually required if a business has a nexus and sells taxable goods or services.

- Assuming you have established procedures to account for sales tax, submit returns, and remit payments to the appropriate authorities, you have a firm grasp on your existing sales tax commitments.
- However, as your business grows and expands, with new employees, additional products/services are offered more sales in states or through mergers/acquisitions. Your nexus and taxability requirements may evolve.
- Make sure to conduct a review of your exposure to determine where you currently stand in terms of nexus and taxability. Having up-to-date knowledge about your obligations is crucial, as this will enable you to effectively manage compliance.
- Set up a billing process that includes applying tax to your invoices. You can. Integrate this functionality directly into your invoicing system. Leverage a third-party sales tax calculation software.
- Implement a system for managing exemption certificates and updating any expired certificates.
- Ensure your sales tax registrations and numbers are current in every jurisdiction where you must pay sales tax. Renew any registrations. Additionally, assign someone the responsibility of monitoring activities that may trigger sales tax obligations requiring registrations.
- Make sure to meet the deadlines for preparing and submitting returns in all the jurisdictions where you have obligations. This could be on an annual basis.
- Have a system to pay the jurisdictions where you are registered for collecting and remitting taxes. Document everything, from purchases to postal receipts.
- Establish a process to handle notices promptly and effectively.
- Keep documentation in case there are personnel changes or turnovers within your organization.
- Ensure you have enough staff members to deal with sales tax audits & nexus questions from the various jurisdictions.

- Maintain a tax calendar that includes any changes in filing frequency methods (paper vs. E file) and payment methods (prepayments, checks or electronic payments).

It is difficult to stay on top of all your sales & use tax commitments. Having the people and processes in place is crucial to ensure compliance and protect yourself and your business from risks.

7.3 Understanding Use Taxes

A "use tax" is a kind of sales tax. This rule applies when a consumer purchases from a country or state that does not impose a sales tax. Whoever purchases products intending to use, store, or distribute them in a state or locality where sales tax is required must do so. Use taxes are levied at the same rate as sales taxes. It is the responsibility of consumers to calculate and pay these use taxes, which can sometimes be challenging to enforce.

Unlike regular sales taxes, which are applied to everything sold, usage taxes are only charged in certain situations. A consumer's home city or state collects this kind of tax in scenarios. Some common examples include.

The seller does not include a sales tax when consumers purchase items outside their jurisdiction. The use tax will apply if the buyer intends to use or store the product in a state or locality that collects sales tax.

In cases where goods are bought from another state, the seller does not charge any sales taxes.

Licensed professionals need to be aware of the use tax if they purchase business supplies in a state or country without a sales tax but plan to use them in a state or country that does impose such a tax. Use taxes are calculated at the same combined state and local rate as sales taxes in the resident's jurisdiction. Consumers are responsible for calculating and paying use taxes for any purchases they make. Residents who fail to pay use tax may face interest and penalties.

Furniture, presents, toys, clothes, automobiles, mobile homes, and airplanes are just some of the things that Californians must pay sales tax on. A California resident must pay sales tax to any store in California if they want to purchase apparel. Remit it to the taxing authorities. In this case, no additional taxes will be owed; however, if these goods were purchased in Arizona, no sales tax is charged and then brought back to California by the buyers themselves or through means, they would need to pay taxes on those goods.

7.4 Use Tax vs. Sales Tax

Use taxes are quite like sales taxes. Goods and services sold in the United States are subject to a sales tax levied by the government and included in the closing price. The seller is responsible for collecting and remitting this to the appropriate authorities.

Local jurisdictions have different sales tax rates. Some states have sales taxes compared to others, while others have no sales tax. Certain states exempt items like food, clothing, and books from sales tax, while others have a tax on all purchases.

The use tax typically follows the rate as the state sales tax. The method of calculation and the person doing the accounting make all the difference. If you make an expenditure and are subject to your state's use tax, you are responsible for calculating how much you owe and remitting that amount to the appropriate authority.

Use tax enforcement is often more difficult than sales tax enforcement. Typically applies to significant purchases of tangible goods.

7.5 Use Tax & Nexus

A nexus is a physical point of contact, such as a storefront or distribution center. However, these examples are not the only ones that fit this description. Even if you do not physically operate in a state, you may still be considered to have nexus there if you have an employee or associate there who generates business for you in return for a cut of the profits. So, how does this concept relate to the use tax?

Purchases made by customers in jurisdictions where the store does not have a physical location often do not require the retailer to collect sales tax. In such circumstances, consumers are responsible for determining the appropriate amount of tax to pay and remitting it to the relevant state agency. A company's obligation to collect sales tax from any jurisdiction is conditional on that country's definition of nexus.

The e-commerce industry's failure to pay sales taxes has led some states to pass laws ensuring that businesses contribute their share. An example is New York implementing Amazon laws, which require retailers like Amazon to pay sales taxes despite not having a presence in the state.

Purpose of Use Tax

The use tax helps prevent unfair competition from out-of-state vendors not required to collect sales taxes. It also ensures that all residents of a state contribute to the funding of state and local programs, irrespective of where they shop. These laws are applicable in states. Not limited to California alone.

Enforcing the use tax can be challenging, as it relies on consumers voluntarily reporting and paying their dues. This means that governments lose money whenever citizens make purchases in tax-free zones. Some states have mandated that online vendors collect taxes whenever their customers purchase to address this issue.

Use Tax Example

Imagine a scenario where someone from California buys clothes online from a retailer based in Oregon. According to Oregon law, the retailer does not charge sales tax on the items. The buyer must still pay a usage tax on the garment purchase to the California Board of Equalization.

On the other hand, if Californians were to buy groceries in Oregon without paying any sales tax, they would typically not owe any use tax since most groceries are not subject to taxation in California.

A Special Gift for Our Readers!

Dear Esteemed Reader,

Thank you for selecting this book. Your choice honors us, and we are excited to be part of your educational and professional journey.

We believe in providing value beyond the pages you hold in your hands. To enhance your learning experience, we have curated exclusive content tailored to complement and enrich the insights shared in this book.

Unlock a World of Exclusive Insights!

By scanning the QR code below, you will unveil a treasure trove of additional resources, tips, and expert insights, meticulously crafted to empower your learning journey.

Dive Deeper into Mastery... Don't miss out!

Chapter 8
Long-Term Tax Planning

Businesses need to prioritize tax planning as a fiscal management strategy. By implementing tax planning strategies, businesses can enhance their tax situation. Attain sustainable financial prosperity.

8.1 Importance of Planning

Tax planning is an important part of sound company management regardless of size or sector. It involves evaluating a business situation and devising strategies to minimize tax obligations while adhering to tax laws and regulations. Engaging in tax planning offers advantages for businesses, including.

- Reduced tax liability: The apparent benefit of tax planning is the ability to decrease a business tax burden. By identifying deductions, credits, and exemptions, businesses can significantly lower the amount they need to pay in taxes. This allows cash to be utilized for essential expenses or invested in the business.
- Better control over cash flow: Efficient tax planning helps companies control their cash flow better. By minimizing their tax liability, businesses have resources to allocate towards expenses or seize growth opportunities. Additionally,

this can facilitate taking advantage of payment discounts or ensuring payments to vendors and suppliers.

- Increased cash flow and reduced tax liability immediately contribute to a company's bottom line. With funds at their disposal for investments or shareholder distributions, businesses are positioned for growth and expansion, leading to profitability.
- In summary, prioritizing tax planning empowers businesses by reducing burdens and providing flexibility in allocating resources towards sustained growth and improved profitability.
- Tax planning plays a role in ensuring that businesses understand and abide by tax laws. This helps them avoid penalties and fines and promotes better compliance.
- Furthermore, tax planning is a risk management tool for companies. By examining their tax situation and identifying issues or areas of concern, businesses can take initiative-taking measures to prevent problems from arising.
- An effective tax planning approach offers businesses flexibility. By reducing their tax liability and improving cash flow, they can seize opportunities as they emerge, invest in growth initiatives, and adapt to the changing market conditions.
- Furthermore, tax planning enhances competitiveness for businesses. They can remain competitive within their markets by reducing tax burdens and enhancing profitability. Recruiting and retaining top talent at market rates requires sufficient capital to invest in the company and reward people.
- Considering these benefits, tax planning ought to be high on every company's to-do list. It not only results in taxes but also improves cash flow, enhances profitability, ensures compliance with regulations, mitigates risks, provides financial flexibility, and boosts competitiveness. Therefore, for businesses, incorporating tax planning into the fiscal management strategy is essential.

By collaborating with the tax experts at Intentional Accounting and utilizing tax planning tactics, businesses can optimize their tax situation and attain sustainable financial prosperity.

8.2 Deferral Tax Strategies

Tax deferral refers to shifting deductions from one year to another or postponing income recognition until a year. It is important to note that tax deferral does not reduce your taxes. It does provide immediate benefits. By implementing these tax strategies and paying fewer taxes upfront each year, you can take advantage of the time value of money. Because of the possibility of earning interest on an investment, a dollar now is worth more than the same dollar in the future.

However, you must put aside some cash for this plan to succeed. Incorporating tax planning through deferral can be a way to save money and optimize your long-term tax situation. Here are six potential strategies you can consider utilizing for tax purposes.

8.3 Retirement Plans

If available, it is smart to participate in a 401(k) or similar company retirement plan. In 2018, you can contribute up to $18,500 to an employer-sponsored 401(k) plan. But if you are fifty or older, you get an extra $24,500 to put in. There was a $500 increase in the contribution limit in 2018. The same contribution limits apply if you have a 403(b)-retirement plan. $18,500 or $24,500.

Your employer provides an IRA option. While it may be considered an alternative to a traditional 401(k), it is still highly beneficial. The contribution limit for this type of IRA is $12,500 or $15,500 if you are fifty or older.

Setting up a 401(k) plan might be worth considering for business owners. If you have workers, it must be either a Safe Harbour 401(k) or a complete conventional 401(k). However, if you are an employee or only have your spouse as an employee, there is an option called Solo 401(k) or Owner 401(k). This choice is cost-effective and highly recommended. On the other hand, if you have employees and want to avoid the expenses associated with 401(k)s, then considering a SIMPLE IRA could be more suitable.

If you are a profitable business owner, a defined benefit plan might be worth considering. Unlike plans this one does not limit your contributions to $24,500. The name "defined benefit" comes from the fact that it is based on the desired benefits you want to receive. If you have workers, you should remember that they need careful thought regarding their insurance. However, I have seen successful business owners take advantage of deductions such as $200,000 or $300,000 through this strategy. If you have workers, you should remember that they need careful thought regarding their insurance.

8.4 Deferring Income, Accelerating Expenses

This tax deferral strategy is quite popular among business owners. Towards the end of December, assessing your year's performance is advisable. If you have had a year, consider moving your January expenses and paying them in advance during the current year. Additionally, try to delay receiving December income as much as possible until January.

If sending out bills in mid-December, it would be wise to wait until January so that the income arrives later. This way, you can defer the income. Expedite the expenses.

8.5 Low Turnover Investments

This is a tax strategy that often goes unnoticed. Every investment vehicle, including mutual funds, index funds, & ETFs, has a "turnover ratio." Most people are familiar with the "expense ratio," which indicates how much the fund costs yearly. These costs reduce your return. It is better to have lower expenses.

When it comes to turnover, a lower rate is preferable because a higher turnover rate implies buying and selling stocks. This indicates that your investment could yield a profit. However, if these investments are in accounts, you must pay taxes on those gains even if you do not receive the money. To efficiently manage your taxes, seeking out stocks with turnover rates is advisable.

Another overlooked consideration is dividend-paying funds compared to those with lower dividends. In your opinion, which one has lower tax implications? Surprisingly, the low dividend-paying fund tends to be more tax efficient because these companies are retaining their profits and causing the stock price to rise significantly.

When it comes to companies that offer dividends, you receive that money. If it is held in a taxable brokerage or other account, you will still be responsible for paying taxes on the money regardless of how you reinvest it. Additionally, the stock price is reduced by that amount. From a tax perspective, I prefer stocks or funds with dividend payments. This way, I can avoid paying taxes on them when I do not want to. It is something to think about and consider carefully.

8.6 Adapting to Regulatory Changes

Regulatory alterations are an occurrence in the life sciences industry as it becomes necessary to adjust to technological advancements, adhere to data privacy laws and ensure the long-term well-being of participants in clinical trials. Nevertheless, complying with these modifications is not always straightforward.

In this chapter, you will discover five strategies for adapting to changes. By embracing a process of managing changes like this, you can anticipate alterations and swiftly and effectively adapt to them. This way, you will safeguard your business from disputes or damage to its reputation.

1. Stay informed about changes.

Regulatory changes do not happen overnight. Before any changes are implemented, consultation, discussion, and debate usually occur. Medical device companies are encouraged to discuss their industry challenges and successes.

Media outlets, specialized content providers, and trade groups like the Association of the British Pharmaceutical Business are good places to learn about developments in the business. The advantages of reading newsletters regularly and going to conferences and seminars are often overlooked.

Businesses can also leverage automation technology to search the internet for keywords of interest. This can help them stay updated on any changes they must be aware of.

2. Create a classification system.

It is important to organize business data to make it easy to categorize, search, update and maintain. When everyone in the organization uses language and terminology, it becomes possible to establish a compliance framework that the entire business can follow.

Many software tools for Governance, Risk and Compliance (GRC) are designed to help businesses adopt language. This helps them efficiently manage their business data and simplifies the process of searching for changes and updates within their datasets.

3. Assign accountability to the chosen person.

Incorporating the duties of change management into an individual's role does not just ensure that they have responsibilities for all compliance activities, but it also serves as a powerful method for businesses to cultivate a pool of skilled professionals. When someone is designated as a compliance officer, they take on levels of responsibility, enhancing their capabilities. This allows them to pool resources from within & outside the firm to solve problems. Provides them with opportunities to update staff members and propose suitable actions. When an employee can take on more responsibilities, everyone wins: the employee, the firm, and the customers benefit from the expanded position.

4. Evaluate the consequences.

Before implementing any changes, it is crucial to assess their impact on the organization's operations. This assessment should consider factors such as risks, mitigations, controls, policy and procedure adjustments and training requirements that would need to be addressed or implemented if the changes are enacted.

The individual responsible for managing organizational changes should take charge of conducting impact assessments. They should involve subject matter experts who can provide insights into the implications of each change for the organization and assist in implementing any necessary measures.

A comprehensive understanding of the consequences of these changes can be achieved by fostering collaboration among departments within the business. This will enable planning for logically addressing them.

5. Implement regulatory changes.

To successfully implement changes, conducting a review across different departments is crucial. The results of this analysis may then be used to design a strategy for putting those changes into effect. It is important to assign action owners and agree upon a timeline to ensure compliance with legislation and regulations before the regulatory change deadline.

The role of the change manager is vital in this process. They are responsible for informing the action owners about their responsibilities and monitoring their progress in fulfilling them. The manager should establish reporting mechanisms to track progress and identify any risks that could affect the timeline.

The regulatory change manager is also responsible for updating information management systems and disseminating information about these changes throughout the organization. It is essential that all departments impacted by these changes fully understand their responsibilities and the consequences of non-compliance.

Chapter 9

Registration for Taxes Around the World and Invoicing

A rundown of the many factors to remember while sending invoices to clients abroad.

9.1 Currency Considerations

When businesses send invoices to customers from countries using widely accepted currencies, like euros, dollars, or pounds, simplifying the process is a practice. One advantage of invoicing and receiving payment in pounds is that there is no risk associated with exchange rates. However, some international clients would rather pay in their currency. Most invoice-based small companies will work with their bank to get forward cover (sometimes called Forward Exchange Contracts) to protect themselves against fluctuations in exchange rates. By doing so, they may avoid monetary loss due to fluctuations in the currency rate while waiting to be paid.

In cases where issuing an invoice is mandatory – for instance, EU regulations stipulate that an invoice must be generated whenever goods are sold, services are provided, or payments are received on account. Invoices can be sent on paper, with all EU member states required to treat both formats. However, sending invoices via email offers benefits such as speed and reducing the likelihood of errors in postal addresses.

When sending invoices, the applicable exchange rate is determined by the kind of products or services being sold and whether the customer is another company or an individual.

You might also need to consider registering for Value Added Tax (VAT). A comparable sales tax in the country where you conduct your business transactions.

9.2 Payment Methods

Once you have decided on the currency you will accept for payment, it is important to consider the methods to receive payments. There are payment options to choose from.

- Bank transfer
- Direct Debit
- Credit/debit card
- Wire transfer
- Digital wallet
- Cheque

Regarding initial investment and continuing expenses, each approach offers benefits and downsides.

To simplify your invoicing process and avoid the stress and expenses associated with payments, you may consider using GoCardless, an automated invoice collection service. GoCardless is easy to set up and ensures that your invoices are paid promptly every time.

9.3 Taxes

Depending on the countries in which you and your customer are situated, taxes and fees might need to be considered. For instance, companies doing business with EU member states must account for VAT while making purchases or sales. When calculating taxes and fees, numerous factors come into play. If you lack expertise in this area, you should seek assistance from an accountant or lawyer.

9.4 VAT issues with EU & international invoicing

You may have to charge value-added tax (VAT) on sales from the United Kingdom to customers abroad. But if you sell anything outside the EU or ship it to someone VAT registered in another EU nation, you do not have to collect VAT on the sale. Remember to verify everything, especially when purchasing used items or transportation. The value-added tax (VAT) normally charged to a non-VAT-registered consumer is instead paid by the VAT-registered customer. Make sure to mention this detail on the invoice. If no VAT is due, that fact should also be noted prominently. Your receipts play a role because HMRC may use them to verify that the products were sent outside the UK (a process known as "evidence of removal"). Enterprises should keep invoices for up to ten years, but only for those registered with VAT Mini One Stop Shop (MOSS), which provides services for firms throughout the EU.

Distance selling

If you are selling products or services to someone not registered for VAT in another European Union (EU) country and it is your responsibility to deliver the goods, then it falls under the category of a distance sale. In this case, as usual, you would charge VAT at the rates in the United Kingdom. However, remember that distance sales have a minimum barrier in each EU nation. For instance, France, Ireland, and Italy have a threshold of 35,000 euros, while Germany, Luxembourg and the Netherlands have thresholds that can go up to 100,000 euros. If your sales value exceeds this threshold in any given country, you must register for VAT in that country and charge your customers based on their VAT rate.

9.5 International invoicing & accurate record keeping

When it comes to invoicing sales, a mechanism called charge often comes into play. This means that the responsibility for reporting the VAT transaction shifts from the seller to the buyer of a product or service. The reverse charge laws aim to streamline commerce by shifting the burden of VAT from the seller to the buyer in transactions between EU member states. However, the seller must indicate that the invoice is "Subject to reverse charge in the country of receipt."

The tax authorities in Britain require businesses that deal with customers to issue VAT invoices that clearly display the VAT amount in pounds and any other currency involved. When updating your accounts, you must record invoices in currencies using the exchange rate on the date of invoicing and convert them into pounds. Even though exchange rates constantly fluctuate, you must keep track of the amount converted into British pounds if you are owed money in currencies. Now, imagine you have sent an invoice to your client in Euros. It has not been paid yet, but the euro value has decreased compared to the pound; you will need to recalculate the amount owed based on this new exchange rate. You will incur a loss due to currency conversion and must include this in your income statement.

When selling to customers from different countries, things can get quite complicated. It is always an idea to consult with an accountant who can help you navigate the various rules and regulations in different jurisdictions. They can also guide you to where you should be paying taxes.

9.6 International Invoice Checklist

Sure, here is the paraphrased text.

- The issuance dates.
- A unique number
- The complete name and address of your company
- Details about the client, including full name and location, and the kind and quantity of the services rendered.
- The date and location where the goods or services were supplied.
- The whole amount due in the designated currency

If you are registered for VAT, and you are sending an invoice to a customer in another EU country, please make sure to include the information.

- Your VAT numbers.
- The customer's VAT number, if
- The rate at which VAT is being charged.
- The amount subject to tax for each rate
- The amount of VAT payable
- If the invoice is in a currency other than sterling, also provide the amount of VAT payable in sterling.
- If the VAT rate on the service you supplied is zero, you must

inform the receiver that they are responsible for paying VAT under Article 44 of the EU VAT Directive.

If you have sold goods and they are subject to a zero-rated VAT rate, state, "VAT exempt according to Article 138 of the EU VAT Directive."

Chapter 10
Managing Tax Disputes and Compliance

10.1 Resolving Tax Disputes

Tax conflicts can put a strain on a company's resources. Recent data indicates that more than 60% of businesses have engaged in tax disputes with HM Revenue & Customs (HMRC) for over a year, highlighting the nature of this problem. There have been concerns regarding HMRC's capacity and timeliness in addressing these disputes, making them increasingly difficult to navigate. Nevertheless, businesses can adopt measures to prevent and effectively manage conflicts.

Understanding the landscape

According to information, three out of every five businesses are engaged in tax disputes with HMRC that have extended beyond a year. This data, encompassing over five hundred businesses, sheds light on the challenges many companies face when navigating the intricate tax system. The latest annual report from HMRC indicates that as of March 31, 2023, there were 39,500 tax tribunal appeals—an increase of 8 per cent compared to the previous year. For businesses undergoing an HMRC inquiry, the average duration for resolving matters—including those that end up in litigation—is approximately 36 months.

Role of ADR

Despite the difficulties involved, businesses have not fully taken advantage of approaches to settling tax disputes. According to the data, although 92 percent of those in dispute with HMRC are aware of ADR options, the utilization rates for ADR remain low. In the 2022/23 period, 1,013 applications for ADR were made.

Through alternative dispute resolution (ADR), certified HMRC mediators collaborate with applicants & the HMRC officer managing their case to brainstorm potential solutions to the conflict. It can be utilized at any stage of a tax inquiry, even after HMRC has decided. Each ADR application is assessed individually. The ADR procedure, which HMRC hopes to wrap up in 120 days, is quicker than the conventional ways of dispute resolution.

Strategies for avoiding and navigating tax conflicts in business.

Try Alternative Dispute Resolution

When a conflict arises, a company should consider whether it may be settled via Alternative conflict Resolution (ADR). ADR has proven to be a means of resolving conflicts, with 87 percent of cases resolved. Delaying the consideration of ADR increases the likelihood of wasted time and the expenses incurred in disputes.

Simplify & modernize.

The tax system can be quite intricate, which sometimes causes confusion and disagreements. To navigate this complexity, businesses should invest in up-to-date accounting software and seek professional guidance to ensure they accurately understand and comply with tax laws.

Stay informed & compliant.

Staying informed about tax laws and regulations can assist businesses in preventing conflicts from arising. Assessing and revising procedures to guarantee compliance with tax laws is essential.

Open communication with HMRC

Maintaining contact with HMRC is essential for solving problems before they escalate into litigation. If a business is uncertain about a tax matter, it is better to ask HMRC or a tax professional for clarification than make an uninformed choice. Tax disputes may be challenging and time-consuming to resolve. Businesses have strategies available to navigate and prevent them.

10.2 Handling Tax Audits

If the IRS audits your business tax return, it means that the IRS is examining whether your business accurately reported all income and claimed the deductions and credits allowed by law.

Audits by the IRS are not conducted at random. The Internal Revenue Service picks returns with the highest mistake rates.

Once you file a return, the IRS has a three-year window to initiate and complete an audit. The IRS sometimes begins auditing tax returns within a year of filing. Completes them in less than a year.

The IRS conducts audits in three ways.

1. by use of a mail audit (correspondence).
2. At the IRS workplace (desk audit)
3. Third, a field audit might be conducted at your residence or business.

For business audits, the IRS opts for in-person field audits. These audits are comprehensive, often examining all aspects of your business as its owner(s). During a field audit, your business records and accounting system will be reviewed, and tests will be conducted to verify income accuracy. On average, completing a business audit can take up to one year. However, businesses can potentially reduce this timeframe by preparing for the audit and promptly responding to any questions or requests from the auditor.

The Internal Revenue Service (IRS) may audit your firm and ask for supporting paperwork and information to help them understand your position. Be careful to provide the IRS with everything it needs in its specified format. If you have enlisted the assistance of a licensed tax professional to manage the audit, make sure to collaborate with them by providing facts which will enable them to communicate with the IRS.

Addressing an IRS business tax audit

To effectively manage a tax audit, it is important to understand its scope.

If you received a mail audit letter from the IRS, it typically focuses on a few items. However, office and field audits require effort. In these cases, you will need to gather the requested information and documents and be prepared to answer questions regarding your business finances and activities. Additionally, you should be ready to explain your business accounting and recordkeeping system.

Handling office and field audits can be challenging if you are unfamiliar with IRS procedures. For help representing yourself and arguing your tax return claims with the IRS, consult a tax expert such as an enrolled agent, CPA, or attorney.

Get ready to answer the IRS's queries.

In case of a mail audit, make sure you provide a response addressing the items mentioned in the letter or document you received from the IRS.

Be ready to meet with an IRS officer and agent in an audit conducted at an IRS office or on the road. Gather all the information that the IRS has requested and be ready to present it to them. Anticipate their questions, such as inquiries about bank deposits or additional income. The IRS representative will also inquire about your employment, family, and any external business ventures. You should be able to provide a comprehensive summary of your year's work.

If you lack documents to substantiate any items on your tax return, you may need to reconstruct those documents using records from parties or other sources. In cases where a third party can vouch for an item technique, like obtaining an affidavit, can be employed.

3. respond to any requests for information or documents from the IRS and defend your position on your business tax return.

If the IRS believes that changes need to be made to your business return, they will ask questions. An IDR, or Information Document Request, will be sent to you to gather details. It is crucial to respond by the given deadline.

The IRS may have opinions, such as claiming that you claimed a deduction that was not allowed or that you should have reported income on your return. If you do not agree, explain to the IRS how the facts and regulations conflict with your position.

The tax audit conducted by the IRS will end, either suggesting no changes or proposing adjustments to your business return. You will receive a report outlining the findings of the IRS along with a letter providing you with 30 days for an appeal if you disagree (referred to as the 30-day letter).

4. If you happen to disagree with the outcomes, you have the option to appeal through the channels.

You can formally request an appeal within 30 days by contacting the IRS Office of Appeals. However, it is important to note that after these 30 days, you will receive a letter from the IRS called a Statutory Notice of Deficiency, which signifies the conclusion of the tax audit process and permits you to take your case to the U.S. Tax Court.

It is worth mentioning that, in mail audits, it is crucial not to overlook or disregard the letter that outlines proposed adjustments, as it also functions as a 30-day notice. Failure to acknowledge this letter could result in losing your right to appeal any audit findings within the IRS system.

A Special Gift for Our Readers!

Dear Esteemed Reader,

Thank you for selecting this book. Your choice honors us, and we are excited to be part of your educational and professional journey.

We believe in providing value beyond the pages you hold in your hands. To enhance your learning experience, we have curated exclusive content tailored to complement and enrich the insights shared in this book.

Unlock a World of Exclusive Insights!

By scanning the QR code below, you will unveil a treasure trove of additional resources, tips, and expert insights, meticulously crafted to empower your learning journey.

Dive Deeper into Mastery... Don't miss out!

Conclusion

"The Guide for Small Businesses on Taxes" was created to help business owners navigate the complexities of the tax code. This book covers concepts, methods and advice that can empower companies to comply with taxes and optimize their success.

Our focus was emphasizing the importance of business owners understanding their tax and legal obligations. By providing an overview of business structures like proprietorships, partnerships, and corporations, we offered readers the necessary tools to evaluate their organization type and grasp the corresponding tax implications.

Additionally, we delved into the intricacies of income tax, sales tax, employment tax and self-employment tax about businesses. We aimed to simplify these concepts so that readers could confidently approach tax preparation reporting and filing. We strived to equip business owners with the knowledge to accurately calculate income claim deductions and promptly fulfil all tax obligations.

Throughout our book, we emphasized using tax preparation as a strategy to minimize tax liabilities while maximizing earnings. We analyzed deductions, credits, and incentives for businesses. This analysis advised our readers to improve their outcomes within legal boundaries.

We also emphasized the need to be organized and keep detailed records. By highlighting documents and key information, we helped business owners streamline their record-keeping practices, making tax preparation more efficient and enabling them to address any IRS audits or inquiries.

Additionally, we recognized not the significance of fulfilling tax obligations but the importance of understanding state and local tax requirements. To ensure that our audience is well informed about tax responsibilities beyond level, we delved into the complexities of trade, nexus considerations and sales tax collection.

Finally, we discussed taxes and other frequent problems encountered by company owners. By addressing topics like contractors, cross-border transactions, payroll management, and tax audits, our goal was to equip you with strategies for tackling these obstacles.

The authors of "The Small Business Guide to Taxes" aimed to empower business owners by guiding them through taxes. The concepts and strategies presented in this book can help business owners ensure compliance while minimizing their tax obligations and maximizing resource allocation. All factors for long-term success.